REFORM THE NIGERIA POLICE

THE INDISPUTABLE WAY FORWARD

PROF. SALIBA DADDY MUKORO

ASPIRE
PUBLISHING HUB LLC.

Reforming the Nigeria Police
Copyright © 2024 by Prof. Saliba Daddy Mukoro

All rights reserved. No part of this publication may be reproduced, distributed, or transmitted in any form or by any means, including photocopying, recording, or other electronic or mechanical methods, without the prior written permission of the author, except in the case of brief quotations embodied in critical reviews and certain other non-commercial uses permitted by copyright law.

Library of Congress Control Number: 2024921514

ISBN
978-1-965318-58-4 (Paperback)
978-1-965318-59-1 (eBook)
978-1-965318-57-7 (Hardcover)

THIS BOOK IS DEDICATED TO MY DEAR COUNTRY:

THE FEDERAL REPUBLIC OF NIGERIA.

TABLE OF CONTENTS

ACKNOWLEDGEMENT	VII
INTRODUCTION	XI
CHAPTER 1. FOUNDATIONAL PROBLEMS OF THE NIGERIA POLICE	1
CHAPTER 2. GROWING THE NIGERIA POLICE IN THE IMAGE OF THE NIGERIAN MILITARY	10
CHAPTER 3. SYSTEMIC CORRUPTION AND COMMAND IMPOTENCE	15
CHAPTER 4. SECURING PUBLIC INVOLVEMENT, TRUST AND SUPPORT FOR THE NIGERIA POLICE	18
CHAPTER 5. RESULTING REFORM STRUCTURES	23
CHAPTER 6. COMBATING ARMED ROBBERY	25
CONCLUSION	29
REFERENCES	30
APPENDIX A	31
APPENDIX B	32
APPENDIX C	33
APPENDIX D	34
APPENDIX E	35
APPENDIX F	36
APPENDIX G	38
ABOUT THE AUTHOR	39

ACKNOWLEDGEMENT

MANY PEOPLE CONTRIBUTED PHYSICALLY or morally to the production of this book - a book some of my colleagues have dubbed "Small but Mighty" (SBM). I must, therefore, thank them generously for their contributions. My thanks first go to my professorial colleagues who either provided editing services, served as bouncing boards to test my ideas about how to effectively reform a National Police System, or provided moral support, in one way or the other, throughout the period it took to write this book, and they include: Professors Emanuel Amadi, Peter Nwankwo, Horace Lyons, Jiabo Liu, Bessie Hutchins, Rochelle Cobbs, Elizabeth Ervin, Anthonio Gaither, John Sutton, Dorothy Jones, Elmus Stockstill, Julius Ikenga, Morgan Ero, Samuel Osunde, Chukwuma Ahanonu, Ademola Omishakin, Takiya Perkins, and Judge Betty Sanders. I thank them all. Thanks also go to Mrs. Caroline Williams, my department secretary, who helped to type the manuscript. My thanks also go to the rest of the faculty, staff, and students of Mississippi Valley State University for their support. Special thanks go to The University President, Dr. Donna Oliver, the University Provost, Senior Vice President, and Chief Operating Officer, Dr. Joseph Stevenson, the Associate Provost, Dr. Samuel Shingles, the Assistant Provost, Dr. Christopher Shults, and the Interim Dean of the College of Professional Studies, Dr. Vincent Venturini, for their unflinching support. My thanks will be incomplete, If I do not very specially thank all the University Presidents, I have worked under in my over forty years in academia, and they are: Dr. Johnson Benjamin

Johnson (R.I.P.), Grambling State University of Louisiana), Dr. Harold W. Lundy (Grambling State University of Louisiana), Dr. William Sutton (Mississippi Valley State University), Dr. Lester C. Newman (Mississippi Valley State University), Dr. Donna Oliver (Mississippi Valley State University), and Dr. Glenell M. Lee-Pruitt (Jarvis Christian University). I greet them all very specially.

To the following special families that happenstance of history have made our paths to cross on positive notes, with me being on the receiving end, I must say thank you from the very bottom of my heart, and the families are: His Eminence, the Sultan of Sokoto, Sa'ad Abubakar III and family, Nobel Laureate, Prof. Wole Soyinka and family, Chief. Odumegwu Ojukwu (The Ikemba of Nnewi) and family, Lt. General A.B. Dambazau and family. Dr. J.O.S. Okeke and family, Dr. Ifeanyi Okpalobi and family, Dr. Odion Ojo and family, Elder Emmanuel Nwosu (R.I.P.) and family, The Excellency of Osun State, former Governor (Prince) Olagunsoye Oyinlola and family, Chief (Dr.) E.K. Clark and family, Mr. Emmanuel Ebe and family, the former and current Governor of my State (Delta State) former Governor, Dr. Senator Ifeanyi Okowa and family, current Governor, His Excellency, Sheriff Oborevwori and family, Mr. Suleiman Jibril and family, Dr. & Dr. (Mrs.) Michael Ogashi, Mr. Adetunla Ayodeji Tosin and family, Mr. Lawson Ajakpovi and family, Major General Barry Ndiomu and family, His Royal Highness of Emevor Kingdom, Dr. John Holt Ologho and Family, Mr. Eyitemi Potokri and family, Mr. Babatunde Gbadamosi and family, Dr. Nurudeen Shekoni and family, High Chief (Dr.) Abel Ubeku (R.I.P), and family, Senator Spanner Okpozo (R.I.P.) and family, Mr. Dominic Oamen and family, Air Commodore David Ashebu (rtd) and family, Brigadier General Alfred Ilogho (rtd) and family, Col. Isah Maina (rtd) and family, Senator Joseph Akaagerger and family, Alhaji Abubakar Hamman Maiduguri and family, Deputy Inspector General of Police, John H. Ahmadu (R.I.P.) and family, Inspector General of Police, MD Abubakar and family, and Chief Sunny Esiso and family. I thank these families very generously. I thank you all.

This book is about the Nigeria Police. I, therefore, must thank all Nigeria Police personnel for all that they do to prevent and control crime in Nigeria. I must particularly thank all the present and past Inspector Generals of the Nigeria Police. I must also, particularly, thank all the past and present Nigerian presidents/Heads of States who have during their tenures made determined efforts to reform the Nigeria police, and they include President Bola Ahmed Tinubu, President Muhammadu Buhari, President Dr. Goodluck Ebele Jonathan, Ex-President Umaru Yar'Adua (R.I.P), Ex-President Olusegun Obasanjo, Ex-Head of State General Abdulsalami Abubakar, Ex-Head of State General Sanni Abacha, Interim Head of State Ernest Shonekan, Ex-President General Ibrahim Babangida, Ex-Head of State Muhammadu Buhari, Ex-President Shehu Shagari, Head of State, General Olusegun Obasanjo, Ex-Head of State General Murtala Mohammed, Ex-Head of State General Aguiyi Ironsi, Ex-President Dr. Nnamdi Azikiwe. I thank them all very generously. I will be remise if I do not also thank the Honorable Distinguished Gentlemen and Women of the Nigeria National assembly for all they do relative to the Nigeria Police, I thank you all.

My military background and upbringing have served me well in all that I do in life. I must, therefore, thank all my military colleagues of the Nigeria Armed Forces, and the commanders I had the opportunity to work with and learn from while in service; these commanders include Lt. General Domkat Yah Bali (R.I.P), Major General Mohammed Gusau, Brigadier General Alabi Isama, Col. Stephen Okoh (R.I.P.) Col. Mesullam Demsa, Col. Phillip Onyekweli, Major General I.O.S. Nwanchukwu, Brigadier General Lawrence Uwumarogie, Brigadier General Idada Ikponwen, Brigadier General Olagunsoye (the former Governor of Osun State of Nigeria, and a proven expert in peace mediation), and many others I may have inadvertently omitted, I send them all my special thanks.

Family members were also very supportive of my efforts in writing this book, and I must thank them generously. To my parents, Chief Stephen Peter Mukoro (R.I.P.) and Chief (Mrs.) Comfort Mukoro

(R.I.P.), I thank them specially from the very bottom of my heart. To my siblings: Sister Florence, Charles, John, Caroline, Peace, Nelson, and Harienth (Oghale) and their respective families, I say thank you. To a special brother, Olugbemi Boye Obasanjo and his family, I send them my very special thanks. To my father and mother-in-laws, Mr. Francis Negbenebor (R.I.P.), and Mrs. Grace Negbenebor (R.I.P), I send my unreserved thanks. To my relations, my uncles, aunties, cousins, nephews, nieces, and their families, my in-laws, and their families, including all others, I say thank you. To my friends all over the world, I say thank you. To my immediate family, my thanks know no limits, to my wife, Chief (Mrs.) Dorah Funmilayo Mukoro (my better half), I say thank you for all the sleepless nights my writing of this book caused you, and the countless hours you devoted to proofreading the manuscripts, including the moral support you accorded me all through this journey. To my sons, Quincy and Lesley, and their families, I say thank you. To my daughters, Stephanie and Jennifer, and their families, I say thank you. To my special daughter Mrs. Karen Imala and her spouse Mr. Ike Imala, and family, I say thank you. To a special son, Joshua Taye Toriola, I say thank you. To the many Nigerians (from North to South, and from East to West) who hold on to the vision that it can no longer be business as usual in our Great Country, and that, Nigeria is, indeed, redeemable, I send my special thanks. Lastly, my Thanks and Glories, which know no limits, go to the Almighty God, through whom all things are possible, including the true reform of the Nigeria Police.

INTRODUCTION

THE NIGERIA POLICE IS IN dire need of reforms designed to reengineer the police establishment for effectiveness. These intended reforms will be inexpensive, groundbreaking, and far reaching. A new Nigeria Police establishment will be born at the end of the reform process. All police officers and other ranks will be happy with their effectiveness, improved welfare, and self-pride; the public will be impressed with the effectiveness and civility of the police; foreign investors will find Nigeria a safe tourist haven and investment destination to invest; and all put together, the dividends of democracy will begin to flow like milk and honey in Nigeria. Though this book is designed specifically for the reform of the Nigeria Police, it is also suitable for the reform of other African Countries police establishments or similarly situated police establishments around the world, particularly the developing Countries.

To realistically reform the Nigeria Police, efforts must first be made to identify the fundamental problems causing the ineffectiveness of the police, and then introduce reforms to address those identified fundamental problems. From the several decades of studying and observing the Nigeria police alongside other police establishments around the world, it is safe to narrow the fundamental problems of the Nigeria Police to the following areas.

1. Foundational problems of the Nigeria Police
2. Growing the Nigeria Police in the Image of the Nigerian Military.

3. Systemic corruption and the attendant command impotence within the Nigeria Police.

4. The long-standing inability of the Nigeria police to secure public support, trust and involvement in the fight against crime and criminals.

This book on "Reforming the Nigeria Police" will discuss these four fundamental problem areas, including the armed robbery problem in Nigeria. Suggested reforms will be proffered after each problem area discussion. Let us now start with the discussion of the foundational problems of the Nigeria police in chapter one.

CHAPTER 1

FOUNDATIONAL PROBLEMS OF THE NIGERIA POLICE

Under the Foundational Problems of the Nigeria Police, the following topics will be covered.

- Coercive origin of the Nigeria Police
- Nigeria Mobile Police versus The Regular Police
- Special Weapons and Tactics (SWAT) Teams
- Regular Police Patrol
- Police Deployment/Spread

• COERCIVE ORIGIN OF THE NIGERIA POLICE

THE NIGERIA POLICE IS AN outgrowth of the Hausa constabulary formed in 1879 in Lagos, the Niger Coast constabulary formed in 1894 in the Niger Delta, and the Royal Niger constabulary formed in 1888 in the North (Country Study and Country Guide, 2004, p.2). These varying constabularies had as their mission the forceful suppression of oppositions to the varying interests of the then colonial masters.

Most of the constabularies were "virtually military in training, in functions, and responsibilities (Kayode, 1976, p.56); they were trained, equipped and psychologically psyched up for their suppressive roles and spent little or no time on protecting the public against crime. When they eventually metamorphosed into the present-day Nigeria police force, their main mission of suppression and coercion was also carried over to the new police force. To date, the Nigeria police has not, in the true sense of the matter, jettisoned this suppressive mission. It is still operationally and structurally molded for public coercion, instead of being an instrument for protecting the public from crime and criminals.

NIGERIA MOBILE POLICE VERSUS REGULAR POLICE

THE NIGERIA POLICE COERCIVE TRADITION gave birth to the "mobile police force"-which is basically a riot control force- and not a regular crime prevention or crime control force. In order to prevent or control crime, the Nigeria police needs regular police patrol units that are public friendly, and thus, able to secure public support, trust, and assistance in crime fighting. No police establishment anywhere in the world has been able to reduce/control crime without the trust, assistance, and cooperation of the population they serve. A riot police unit, such as the "mobile police force' of the Nigeria police, is characterized by aggression, coercion, and attracts public hate. For example, in Nigeria, they have earned the name "Kill and Go", because of the frequent killings of innocent citizens. To continuously use them for crime prevention and control duties is to forever bid fare well to the ability to solve crime and achieve a peaceful society in Nigeria. How have other effective police agencies in the world dealt with the issue of Riot Policing and Crime Prevention/Control Policing? They have, for the most part, reduced the visibility of Riot police to the public and increased the visibility of regular police patrols designed to prevent, control, and combat crime. They have achieved this by forming SWAT (Special Weapons and Tactics) teams within their police units.

• SPECIAL WEAPONS AND TACTICS (SWAT) TEAMS

The SWAT teams consist of personnel of each police unit, who come together, in special anti-riot uniforms and gears, to handle riots and situations calling for special weapons and tactics. As soon as the business is taken care of, they take off their SWAT uniforms (similar to the mobile police uniforms and gears), and revert to their regular police uniforms and regular patrol duties to prevent and control crime. The advantage of this system is that the public will see them in their coercive uniforms for a brief period of time only and, therefore, does not leave a lasting impression of coercion on the public's mind that will arouse negative feelings towards the police, and thus, translate to lack of support and cooperation with the police. It is also more cost effective to use the same body of men for regular police duties, such as patrol functions, which requires civility, and then also be able to use them for riot control (requiring coercion) only when needed. Riots or violent disturbances happen infrequently, and to keep a riot force, such as the mobile police continuously is an expensive and wasteful venture. To use them for regular crime prevention/control duties with all the animosity they attract is share waste of time and effort, as public support, and community involvement will not be forthcoming. It is general knowledge that crime can only be reduced / controlled with community involvement. The community cannot be involved with an unfriendly force which they generally refer to as "Kill and Go" squads. To even go further and talk about implementing community policing under this dispensation is un-thinkable and certainly doomed to fail no matter the resources devoted to the effort.

ATTENDANT REFORM RECOMMENDATION

1. Disband Mobile Police Units and redeploy their personnel to regular police units. They may serve as members of their respective new units SWAT Teams, if selected. To save cost, they may go with their uniforms and kits to their new units to be used for SWAT Team duties only (which are occasional). For all other times, they will be involved in regular police patrol duties in their regular police uniforms.
2. SWAT Teams (Special Weapons and Tactics) teams should be formed in all police units to respond to riots and special conditions requiring force and special weapons. At the end of each SWAT operation, the SWAT members will return to their normal regular police uniforms and duties, including regular police patrols to prevent and control crime.

REGULAR POLICE PATROL

REGULAR POLICE PATROL

THE FOUNDATION OF THE NIGERIA police, as already indicated, emphasized the forceful suppression of oppositions to the then colonial masters. The emphasis was on a strong coercive force, and thus resulted in the development of the coercive mobile police concept. Since there was little or no emphasis on crime prevention and control, no real effort was made to develop or build the regular police patrol aspect of the Nigeria police. Patrolling is an important aspect of policing required for preventing and controlling crime. With the shift of the Nigeria Police to now emphasizing crime prevention and control, it also becomes necessary to now build a strong regular police patrol contingent of the Nigeria Police to regularly provide 24 hours patrol of the communities people reside in, as the mobile police concept is not suitable for crime prevention and control, but for quasi military operations where use of force is required.

ATTENDANT RECOMMENDATIONS

3. Regular police patrol duties should be elevated to top priority in the Nigeria police.

4. Sixty to sixty five percent of all police operational units personnel are to be assigned to regular police patrol duties covering three shifts (morning shift-6:00 a.m. to 2:00 p.m.; evening shift-2:00 p.m. to 10:00 p.m.; night shift-10:00 p.m. to 6:00 a.m.)

5. Patrol and shift duties should be made compulsory for all officers and other ranks of the Nigeria Police. While patrolling is the most important function of policing, shift duties ensure that police personnel are available at all times.

6. To emphasize the importance of patrol, all new police recruits should start as patrol officers (instead of constables). All present serving constables should now be referred to as police officers (PO), and a befitting insignia should be designed for this new position/rank. This should bring respectability to these officers who are constantly in contact with the public, as they do their jobs.

POLICE DEPLOYMENT SPREAD

POLICE DEPLOYMENT/SPREAD

The desire to protect the colonial master's interests (which were mainly located in the towns and cities) led to the traditional deployment of police units/resources in just towns and cities where only 25% of the Nigerian population reside (Country Guide and Country Studies,

2002, p.1), leaving the rest of the nation, where 75% of its population reside, without meaningful police coverage. To date, this 75% of the population have no police presence or, in some cases, have police posts comprising mostly of junior police personnel who are easily pocketed by criminal elements. They, thus, dine and wine with the criminals at will and begin to protect and work actively with criminals. Under this dispensation, crime is bound to remain a problem no matter how much is spent on the Nigeria police. Crime displacement theory also posits that criminals will be displaced from well policed areas to less policed areas (Cole and Smith, 2001). In the Nigerian scenario, the villages and suburbs where a total of 75% of the Nigerian population reside serves as breeding grounds for criminals, as the lack of police presence in full force, proffers them the freedom to breed, recruit and train criminals unhindered. They then travel to towns and cities for criminal activities and then return to the villages where they are undisturbed.

• ATTENDANT RECOMMENDATION

1. Enough police officers and men should be posted from city and town police commands to the villages to make sure that each Nigerian village has a small size police department with a police chief not below the rank of an Assistant Superintendent of Police (ASP). The village police chief should have the same responsibilities as the police chiefs in local government area city/town police departments, such as, the provision of police patrols throughout the village in 3 shifts (6:00am to 2:00pm, 2:00pm to 10:00 pm, and 10:00 pm to 6:00 am); maintain records of guest sign in sheets in all hotels in their jurisdictions, so as to identify suspicious guests in need of police surveillance if they are found attempting to commit criminal acts, they can be stopped before the commission of the act (s), similar to best police practices in other effective police establishments around the world; maintain up-to-date records from landlords about their tenants and their occupations, so as to identify those without jobs but are leaving

above their means, and, therefore, subject to police surveillance (after the appropriate judicial approval); ensure adequate welfare of all police personnel; develop activities to foster good police and community relations etc.. Carrying out of these practices in all Nigerian villages will ensure that criminals will no longer have the luxury of un-policed areas to breed, train, recruit or operate freely without being caught before acting. This reform will result in all areas (100%) inhabited by all Nigerians having full effective police coverage. This move will drastically increase police effectiveness and thus reduce crime rates tremendously. Nigerians would then be able to travel from one part of the country to the other, both during the day and night, without the fear of crime, whatsoever.

2. All village police department should be equipped with at least 2 cars for 24 hours patrol, one police car for the police chief, at least 2 pool cars for the use of the investigation section, for the crime intelligence and surveillance section, and other sections of the department. The department should be located in a befitting office bungalow, with a duty room and a lock up cell attached. There should also be communication medium from the police duty room to all the police vehicles, and to all police personnel on duty through walkie-talkies. Additional funds may not be required to meet these needs. If all the areas of wasteful and unproductive expenditures that currently exist in the Nigeria police are cut, enough funds would be saved to cater for these vehicular, communications, and office space needs.

3. Policing by local government areas:

The most senior police officer in a local government area is the Divisional Police Officer (D.P.O.). This concept and the title are outdated. The title of D.P.O. (Divisional Police Officer) does not connote command authority, and also not empowering. The weight of the law Enforcement responsibilities fall squarely on the shoulders of the Divisional Police Officers. They are the ones that command the police personnel doing the day to day police work, and who are in contact with the public on a day-to-day basis. Practically, their position is about the most significant and critical operational command position in the Nigeria Police. It is, therefore, crucial to recognize their importance and address them appropriately as **Police Chiefs**, as is the practice in most of the effective police departments around the world, including the United States of America. They should be responsible for policing the towns or cities where the local government headquarters are located and other remote villages in the local government area (if any) will have small size police departments with their respective police chiefs and their personel drawn from their local government police personell holding. All the police chiefs in a local government area will be directly and singularly responsible for preventing and controlling crime in their jurisdictions, and **are directly answerable to their State Police Commissioners,** and shall be **funded directly from the Inspector General of police through the State Commissioners of Police based on budgets prepared and defended by them.** The present situation where the D.P.O.s (Divisional Police Officers) are responsible for all the villages in their local government area is ineffective and a colonial legacy. For the sake of accountability, each city, town, or village must be independently policed, where the respective Police Chiefs are held accountable for the crime rates in their jurisdictions. The respective police chiefs will be commended if they maintain low crime rates in their jurisdictions, and remove from command if they allow crime rates to remain high in their jurisdictions. Funding their police departments directly will ensure that they get all the resources they need to do a good job. The issue of no vehicle to pursue criminals or to respond to calls for police service, or no battery, or no tire, or no petrol will be a thing of the past. The respective police chiefs should be empowered and given the resources they need to do their job, including attractive salaries. They should also participate in recruitment exercises. The present system of centralized recruitment is now outdated and no longer productive. It is better for **each police chief to recruit their men and women with proper detailed background checks and federal character compliance.** They will then send their recruits to the police College for basic police training. The trained recruits will return to their sending units on completion of their training. By so doing, no police chief will blame the police hierarchy for recruiting bad police persons, including armed robbers for them. **When these police chiefs are properly empowered with befitting titles, budget, power to hire and dismiss, they will have no excuses for failure.** If they keep crime rates low in their jurisdictions they will get the credit; if they allow crime rates to get out of hand, their jobs will be on the line. The present situation where police commanders remain unperturbed even when crime rates reach the sky would be a thing of the past. Without this type of accountability requirements, police commanders will not bring out the best in themselves and their personnel. Productivity should be the key. Unproductive officers and the rank and file should have no place in a reformed Nigeria police.

CHAPTER 2

GROWING THE NIGERIA POLICE IN THE IMAGE OF THE NIGERIAN MILITARY

THE MANY YEARS OF MILITARY rule in Nigeria resulted in the Nigeria police building itself in the image of the military — doing everything like the military. What is good for the military might not necessarily be good for the police. While the main similarity between the military and the police is that they both wear uniforms, they are different in many other aspects. For example, while the military has a very long period of peace-time soldiering (when there is no war) with ample time for all forms and shapes of training to occupy the free time, the police do not have that luxury. The police are all the time combating crime (there is no peace time). To line the police up for military natured courses like the Nigerian Defense Academy type Nigeria Police Academy, a five year course (Library of Congress, Nigeria Police Force, 1991, p.3), Command and Staff College type courses, and other similar military type courses, with no direct relationship to police duties amounts to monumental waste of resources, that are urgently needed to procure police equipment, improve police salaries, welfare and to fund short duration police related courses, such as police management courses, criminal investigations, police patrol courses, crime intelligence courses, surveillance courses, dog handling courses, forensic courses, basic training courses, etc. These courses are directly related to police duties, and directly enhance police job performance. It is too expensive to take a police officer off the street to do a long duration course that has no direct relationship to his or her police job. This trend, even though well intentioned, continues to hamper Nigeria police overall performance since the years of military rule to date. The resources presently used to run these long-duration military type courses, and the upkeep of such training institutions ought to be used to equip the police from village to village, town to town, and city to city, to the point that the entire nation will have full police coverage (100%), where nothing moves, shakes, or drops, without it being noticed by the police, such as is the case in other well policed societies. Furthermore, the police do not have the luxury of time, as does the military in peacetime, to spend on long courses. They need all the time they can get to combat crime on the streets on a daily basis.

• ATTENDANT REFORM RECOMMENDATIONS

• Training

ALL COURSES THAT HAVE NO DIRECT relationship to police duties should be scrapped, and the training institutions closed down. The infrastructures should be sold to the highest bidder, or converted to other productive governmental or private sector uses. The running costs and proceeds from the sales of such infrastructures should be used to equip police units with patrol vehicles, communication equipments, befitting office accommodations, and to enhance the salaries and allowances of all police personnel. In the United States of America where the police system is effective, their police officers and the rank and file, for the most part, attend short duration courses, lasting a few days, or a few weeks, or a few months, and yet, the police departments in the United States are some of the bests in the world. Their basic training for new recruits has an average duration of between 2 weeks to 16 weeks (Cole and Smith, 2001, p. 206). Some of the longest and most prestigious courses for U.S. police officers are averagely between 2 to 3 months courses at the Federal Bureau of Investigation Academy (Federal Bureau of Investigation Academy Web Page, 2004). There is no such thing as sending a police officer to a police academy for five years pursuing a university degree (Library of Congress, Nigeria Police Force, 1991, P. 3), or to a command and staff college for a one-year course. It is more cost effective to recruit university graduates into the Nigeria Police than to produce them in-house at an alarming cost. Such resources ought to be used to fund additional patrol cars, forensic labs, communication gadgets, befitting office accommodations, surveillance equipment, increased police salaries and allowances, etc.

- **Hierarchy**

While the military performs best under strong hierarchical order, the police performs best under a decentralized command structure for example, almost all military operations involve the movement of a large body of men. It is, therefore, essential to have an effective chain of command to ensure that all efforts are coordinated at each level towards the same objectives and goals, and that all movements of all units are synchronized to ensure no unit runs into other units and thus become casualties of friendly fire, and also, to ensure that no unit due to sluggishness is allowed to bug down the swift advance of the main force. All these maneuvers require hierarchical coordination from the top to the bottom in order to be an effective fighting force, and these are manifested in hierarchical levels of command such as battalion command level, brigade command level, Division Command level, and the Army command level. However, for the typical police establishment, there is no need to move a large body of men in their day-to-day operations, instead their operations are localized in a particular location i.e. in a city, town, or village as the case may be, and it is the local police commander who directs the police operations in the particular city, town, or village. For example, the local commander determines how many patrol cars to be sent out on patrol, who should be assigned to conduct investigations in the cases reported to the police and determines the type of crime prevention strategies to be utilized. In other words, the local commander determines how best to tackle the crime problem within his or her jurisdiction. The only necessary input from the top (hierarchy) is the supply of resources for the local police commander to do his or her job. Since the hierarchy plays only a small part in the whole crime fighting equation, it is counterproductive to create a long hierarchical chain similar to that of the military (where the hierarchy is fully involved in all phases of battles, and to some extent directly or indirectly commands the operations). Furthermore, unlike the military where the missions, goals and objectives are the same and suitable for hierarchical command, the police, for the most part, have different missions, goals, and objectives depending on their localities of operations. For example, each location has its own unique problems to be policed. While a police unit in a village in Sokoto state may have the main problem of battling cattle thieves, the police unit in the Delta may be battling crude oil bunkering, and yet the unit in Benue State may be battling agricultural product thefts. The different nature of problems facing different police units make it impossible for hierarchical command style, similar to that of the military, to work in a police operation type environment. Localized control becomes the typical solution. The availability of the needed resources and the duty consciousness of the localized police commanders and unit personnel, and their rapport with their community determine their level of effectiveness in crime prevention and control. Since no large bodies of men are to be moved typical of the military, and since police units do not have oneness in objectives like the military, but differing and multi-faceted objectives, there is, therefore, no need to build an elaborate hierarchical structure like the military in the police establishment. Such structures in the context of the police are unnecessary, wasteful, and unproductive. For example, while the army has four divisional level commands, the police reform introduced under military governments in 1986 and 1989 (Country Study and Country Guide, Nigeria Police Force, 2004, P.3-4), introduced 12 divisional equivalent command levels into the Nigerian Police called "zonal commands", commanded by Assistant Inspector Generals of Police.

• Zonal Commands

The localized nature of policing does not require these hierarchical commands, they create unwanted bureaucratic bottlenecks, and make commanding the police a difficult task for the Inspector General of police, as he or she will not be able to have direct and timely contact with each state police command to read the crime situation and meet their demands for resources on a timely basis. Without any doubts, the zonal commands are operationally and administratively unnecessary. The cost of funding the zonal commands can equip several cities, towns, and village police departments with police patrol cars, police operational technological gadgets, including communications that will dramatically improve the crime prevention and control abilities of the Nigeria police.

All the 12 police zonal commands should be scrapped for good. They are concepts borrowed from the military and are of no productive value for police type operations, and are unnecessary bureaucratic bottlenecks and clogs in the wheel of police operational and administrative effectiveness, and a monumental waste of police scarce resources.

CHAPTER 3

SYSTEMIC CORRUPTION AND COMMAND IMPOTENCE

WHILE THERE ARE GOOD MEN and women of honor in the Nigeria Police, the bad eggs in the police, amongst the officers and the rank and file, have given the Nigeria police a bad name when it comes to corruption. It is now common knowledge amongst Nigerians that corruption in the Nigeria police is pervasive and systemic. The "whetting you get for me" and "whetting you bring for me" syndrome of the Nigeria Police cannot be denied. It does not end with the rank and file. Many officers are deeply involved. Some are alleged to receive returns from the rank and file (proceeds from check point collections, proceeds from bribes, proceeds from outright cooperation with criminals, and at times, proceeds from direct criminal activities). The involvement of police officers in these schemes with the rank and file over the years have crippled the ability of many police officers to effectively command or discipline police personnel, and I refer to this state of powerlessness as "Command Impotence". You cannot be involved in illegal and corrupt deals with police personnel over the years and expect to still be able to exercise effective command and control over them. It is reasonable to assume that these unholy corrupt relationships are pervasive and systemic in the Nigeria police, and it is beginning to affect the ability of the police officer's corps to effectively command and control their rank and file. There is an urgent need to revise this trend. The crucial level of police command, as already indicated, is the Divisional Police Officer's level. They are the ones in the fore front commanding the efforts to fight crime and interacting with the community. It is, therefore, important that all efforts must be made to identify only the honorable officers within the Nigeria police to fill the D.P.O positions (now recommended to be called Police Chiefs) due to the importance of their roles. Additionally, it is also necessary to mass produce new officers from our burgeoning army of unemployed university graduates (after meticulous background checks), including our graduates abroad, give them three months of condensed training, decorate those with bachelor's degree with the rank of Deputy Superintendent of Police or any other appropriate rank, and those with master's degrees with the ranks of superintendent of police or any other appropriate rank, and bring them in as reform agents. Some should be deployed in addition to other identified honorable officers already in the Nigerian Police to take over the DPO commands in the cities, towns, and village police commands. If they are many enough, they will effectively neutralize the effect of the systemic corruption and the attendant command impotence presently plaguing the Nigeria police and evolve a new police officer and rank and file culture, devoid of corrupt practices, where police productivity and reduced crime rates will be the norm of operational work and upward mobility within the reformed Nigeria police.

• ATTENDANT REFORM RECOMMENDATIONS

1. Comprehensively screen all DPO's and weed out the corrupt and unproductive ones.
2. Replace some of the removed corrupt DPO's with selected officers of integrity within the Nigeria Police.

3. Recruit enough civilian graduates (from within and outside the country) and provide them with condensed 3 months training that covers police administrative skills, police operations to include patrol, investigations, surveillance, traffic, and budgeting duties, etc., to take over some DPO positions. They will be brought in as reform and change agents and will help to neutralize the systemic corrupt culture that is presently pervasive in the Nigeria police, and thus help reverse the prevalent "Command Impotence" presently plaguing the Nigeria Police.

CHAPTER 4

SECURING PUBLIC INVOLVEMENT, TRUST AND SUPPORT FOR THE NIGERIA POLICE

POLICE ESTABLISHMENTS CANNOT SUCCEED IN combating crime without the support and involvement of the community they serve. In order to improve the Nigeria police relationship with the community, and thus be able to secure the public's respect, trust, and support for its operations, the following five measures need to be undertaken.

- Re-designation of police units as per the names of cities, towns, or villages they serve.

- Moving from coercive approaches to friendly and persuasive approaches

- Improving police uniform appearance and rank nomenclature at the constable level

- Improving police salaries

- Gradual phasing out of police barrack accommodations, paying police personnel realistic housing allowance to be able to live amongst the people they serve.

A. **Re-designation of Police Units as per the Cities, Towns, or Villages they serve:** If police units are named after the locality they serve, it will more likely than none, improve the locality's acceptance of the police unit. They will view them as their own, to be supported, liked, and involved with. For example, a police unit serving Shagamu town should be referred to as Shagamu Police Department. The police unit serving the city of Warri should be called Warri Police Department. And all the patrol cars should similarly bear the names of their localities in which they are operated in. For example, a police patrol car in Zaria, should have Zaria Police Department (ZPD) printed on both sides of the car, while the rear bumper and the license/number plate should read "Nigeria Police" (see Appendix D and E for some examples). The word "force" should be eliminated, as being no longer necessary in modern democratic policing dispensations. This re-designation system will also improve police accountability. Presently, police personnel in police vehicles can move from one part of the country to another to perform illegal duties and remain unidentifiable. With this recommended system, the public or police authorities will be able to trace the identities of police vehicles and easily identify where they come from. If a Sapele Police Department patrol comes into Warri to perform illegal duties, the populace will immediately know to inform the police authorities, as it will be clear that such patrol car do not belong to their city or town and, therefore, has no business being there, unless it is in hot pursuit of criminal elements. It is clear that re-designation of police units as per the communities they serve will improve accountability on the part of police personnel, and will improve police community relations, as the community will see the police units as their own to be supported and involved with.

B. **Moving from Coercive Approaches to Friendly and Persuasive Approaches:** A police unit devoid of coercion and, instead, utilizes more friendly and persuasive approaches stands a better chance of securing support and cooperation from the community they serve. This re-orientation can be achieved and taught to police personnel during trainings and reemphasized on the job daily.

1. **Improving Police Personnel Uniform Appearance and Rank Profile:** The look of a police uniform on police personnel can either attract respect or disrespect from the public depending on the quality and look of the uniform. A police personnel in a well-tailored uniform, with nice shoulder barges (reflecting the community they serve on one shoulder, and Nigeria police on the other shoulder), with a belt affixed with police gadgets, such as walkie-talkie, night stick, revolver, torch light, handcuffs, etc., will attract genuine respect and support from the public than a rag tag police officer with horrible looking uniform and an empty belt lacking policing gadgets. Pistols or revolvers are the police personal weapons of the twenty-first century. Rifles should not be seen with police personnel on the street, except when on special operations as a member of a swat team. The share weight of a rifle will fatigue even the strongest police personnel when carried around as personal weapon. Furthermore, the long range of rifle fire, which is upward of 200 to 300 meters, make it unwise to use them in populated areas without causing collateral damages to innocent bystanders. The constable rank will not attract the same public respect and cooperation as police personnel referred to as a patrol officer, particularly if patrolling is to be regarded as the core of police work in the reformed Nigeria Police. Similarly, Patrol Officer (PO) should replace the constable rank. The word "officer" is more dignifying and more likely to attract public respect, cooperation, and support for personnel at that rank level.

2. **Improving Police Salaries:** Police officers and men have no "peace time", they are always at war battling crime and

criminals. Their lives can be snuffed out at any moment. The very high-risk factors (hazards) that go with the policing profession must be compensated for in how much they are paid (salaries). The police officers and the other ranks must be well paid. A university graduate that enters the police should earn more than the average pay of their graduate counterparts in the civilian work force. The same should apply to high school graduates in the Nigerian Police. Nigerian police personnel must earn good and respectable salaries and allowances to shield them from corrupt temptations and secure the respect and support of the public.

3. **Gradually Phase-Out Barrack Accommodations and Cause Police Personnel to Live Amongst the People they Serve:** The housing of police personnel in barracks is an outdated concept and works against good police community relations. The public is better served when police personnel live in their midst. For example, it is easier to pass information on criminal activities to your neighbor who is a police person than to go to the barracks to pass such information. Police personnel are better able to know what is happening in their communities when they live in them as opposed to when they live outside of them. Additionally, bureaucratic problems involved in providing accommodation and maintaining them, including the exorbitant costs involved can all be avoided if police personnel leave outside of barracks. As a consequence, police personnel should be given monthly rent allowances at the prevailing market rates in their localities of residence.

ATTENDANT REFORM RECOMMENDATIONS

1. Re-designate police units and their patrol cars as per the community they serve.

2. Re-orientate Nigerian Police personnel to move from coercive approaches to friendly and persuasive approaches, and using force only when necessary.

3. Improve police uniform appearance with befitting gadgets and replace rifles as police personal weapons with pistols, and revolvers, except for SWAT teams on special, but infrequent operations, and when in direct combat against rifle carrying terrorists or violent criminals.

4. Replace the rank of constable with patrol officer (PO) or just police officer (PO).

5. Enhance police salaries. They should earn more than their counterparts in the civilian workforce (because of the high-risk factor that go with their jobs, and their importance in ensuring a peaceful safe environment that would allow other career obligations in the society to thrive, and the importance of discouraging corruption).

CHAPTER 5

RESULTING REFORM STRUCTURES

AT THE END OF THE reform exercise of the Nigeria police, the following structures should be evident in the Nigerian Police.

1. Nigeria Police National and State Headquarters Organizational Structures (see Appendix A& B), and for the recommended personnel for City/Town, and Village Police Departments (see Appendix D & E).
2. For a possible view of a police patrol car designated as per the locality it serves (see Appendix F& G).

Nigeria Police Manpower Calculation

- Police manpower and resources should also be allocated per local government areas. For example, each local government area should have at least 350 police personnel (see appendix B) as follows.
- The 350 personnel police departments should be located in each local government area.

- A unified city police department may be formed by combining all the police personnel of the different local governments within the city areas into one large, unified police department under a chief of police.

- Other villages in the local government areas will each have small size village police departments of approximately 48 personnel (se Appendix E), may be scaled down or up depending on the population size of the villages.

- 350 personnel × 774 local governments = 270, 900 (total Strength of Nigeria Police after reform) plus another 5000 to staff police headquarters, state police command headquarters police training institutions, airports, ports, university campuses etc., and another 40, 600 to establish village police departments as per appendix E. The sum of 270, 900 + 5000 +40,600 = 312, 200 (Balogun, Tafa. This Day News, P.2, Feb.19, 2004). In other words, we have enough police personnel to provide 100% police coverage down to the village levels, as opposed to the present situation where police personnel do all they can to remain bunched up in cities and towns.

CHAPTER 6

COMBATING ARMED ROBBERY

ARMED ROBBERY IN NIGERIA is now a daily and deadly menace. While efforts to find a lasting solution have not yielded the required results, it is strongly believed that the comprehensive and meticulous implementation of all the Nigeria Police reform recommendations discussed in this chapter will deal a big blow to the armed robbery gangs and thugs in Nigeria. For example, if all the cities, towns, and villages have full and effective police coverage, we would have achieved 100% coverage as opposed to the present 25% coverage (Country Study and Country Guide, 2003, P.1). With the full 100% coverage, there will be no vacuum for armed robbers to freely operate, recruit, multiply, and grow. The recommended new emphasis on regular police patrol will also ensure that cities, towns, villages, and the highways are saturated with police patrols (cars, motorcycles, bicycles, and foot patrols). The new and real emphasis on crime intelligence will ensure that criminals are ferreted out before they strike. The crime intelligence personnel will be well funded to be able to directly or indirectly infiltrate criminal groups all over the length and breadth of the country. Furthermore, if only men and women of proven integrity are appointed police chiefs of cities, towns, and village police departments, and are held accountable for the crime rates in their jurisdictions, these police chiefs will ensure that the present fraternization of some police personnel with criminals, to the point of looking the other way when the armed robbers rob, maim, and slaughter their victims, or even collaborate with them in the acts, will no longer be tolerated, as they the police chiefs will know that their jobs will be on the line if such acts are allowed to continue, or if crime rates in their jurisdictions are not permanently kept low, as it will no longer be acceptable for crime rate to be sky high and police chiefs will be blaming everybody but themselves, and explaining the unexplainable, and yet not get punished. With these recommended reforms, all such actions will be immediately sanctioned. Police chiefs will owe their jobs to their ability to keep crime rates, including armed robbery rates in their jurisdictions perpetually low.

The recommended direct funding of police departments based on budgets prepared and defended by them, will ensure that they have all the resources they need to be effective in combating all crimes, including armed robbery, corruption, terrorism, etc. In the same vein, if the police departments are re-designated as per the names of the cities, towns, and villages they serve, the public will see these departments as more of theirs and will result in a better flow of information and support from the public to the police. This information flow will steadily increase when the public realizes that the reforms have brought credible police chiefs into office all across the country. The usual fear of furnishing information to the police, and then the police turn around and inform the criminals about the informants will no longer be there. The intended reforms will also terminate the public anger and bitterness towards the mobile police (because of their standing record of public coercion that have earned them the nick name "kill and go"), as there will be a transition from the outdated mobile police force concept to the modern SWAT concept. This foundational concept change will witness tremendous increase in public support for the new Nigeria Police, and thus, should open a flood gate of public information flow to the police, which will in turn lead to apprehension and prosecution of more criminals, including armed robbers.

Additionally, since the police chiefs all over the country will be directly involved in police recruitment and background checks under the reformed policing dispensation, there will be no excuse for recruiting armed robbers or persons with unholy character into their command/ the Nigerian police. This will additionally be a big blow to the armed robbery gangs and other criminals operating in Nigeria.

THE ONLY MISSING LINK: THE DEATH PENALTY

FOR ARMED ROBBERY

Prior to the introduction of the death penalty as a sanction for armed robbery, armed robbery incidents used to be less violent. For example, it was common then to see a person who has just driven off in his or her car coming back on foot complaining that his or her car has been taken at gunpoint by armed robbers. Since the introduction of the death penalty, such nonviolent robbery incident no longer exists. The norm now is violent and deadly robberies. Today's armed robbers, in a bid to avoid the death penalty, will kill off all their victims, including passers by to ensure no one is alive to testify against them in the courts/ tribunals. In other words, the death penalty sanction has tremendously caused an increase in the violence attributable to armed robberies in present times, than in the days when the death penalty was not the prescribed sanction for armed robbery. This supports the "brutalization effect" hypothesis in criminology, which postulates that harsh and brutal sanctions (such as the death penalty) evoke extreme levels of brutality in offenders (Cochran et al., 1994, P.1).

Apart from the violence that the death penalty for the offense of armed robbery attracts, it is also clear that this harsh punishment contributes to the failure of the public to squeal on armed robbers to the police. For example, law abiding citizens will shy away from informing the police about the identities of armed robbers for the fear that such reports will lead to the execution of those reported and that their blood will be on their (the reporters) heads. On the other hand, if the sanction for armed robbery was to be ten to fifteen years in prison, more people will be more willing to report or reveal the identities of armed robbers they know of to the police for prosecution, believing that the prison sentence will correct their wrong ways. If this becomes the case, even relations will squeal on their relatives, knowing that they will not be executed but imprisoned to correct their bad ways. Any option that will improve free flow of information from the public to the police about armed robbery perpetrators must be encouraged to aid in winning the war against the armed robbery menace in Nigeria.

- **ATTENDANT REFORM RECOMMENDATIONS**

1. The comprehensive and meticulous implementation of all the recommended reform measures in this reform book will bring Nigeria out of the armed robbery quagmire she is presently enmeshed in, including other forms of criminalities in Nigeria.

2. The federal government should look into the possibility of scrapping the death penalty for armed robbery to reduce the present state of violence that go with robbery incidents and to make the public more apt to report on armed robbers to the police.

3. A prison sentence of twenty years should be recommended as the sanction for armed robbery. By the time an armed robber spends twenty years in prison; he or she would have outgrown the criminality prone age and will not be a problem to society on release (Cole and Smith, 2001).

4. If in the course of committing an armed robbery offense, the armed robber(s) kill their victim(s), the armed robbers will be charged for armed robbery (which carries a prison sentence), and they will also be charged with murder, which may lead to the death penalty or life imprisonment. This will force armed robbers to run away from killing their victims and thus result in a tremendous reduction of violence, and protection of lives.

CONCLUSION

THIS REFORM BOOK TOUCHED ON areas militating against the Nigeria police effectiveness. Some of the problems were traced to origin of the Nigeria police; to growing the police in the image of the military; to the endemic systemic corruption and the resultant command impotence plaguing the Nigeria police; to the police inability to secure public support in its fight against crime and criminals; and of course, to the daily and deadly armed robbery menace in Nigeria.

Far-reaching recommendations are proffered immediately following each of the discussed areas. A comprehensive and meticulous implementation of the recommended reforms will, without doubts, produce a new Nigeria Police that will be transiting from **neo-colonial** policing to **modern policing** of the twenty-first century. This will be the pride of the Nigeria Police, all Nigerians, Investors, Tourists, and, on a larger scale, the Committee of Nations. To shy away from taking far reaching and, perhaps, drastic decisions, to correct the long-standing anomalies in the Nigeria police, no matter who's ox is gored, will serve no useful purpose. The time to correct the wrongs and develop a police model befitting the twenty-first century is now. For sure, this will be one of the lasting legacies of the democratic dispensation we now enjoy as a nation that is destined to be great. This reform model is also suitable for the State Police concept. All that needs to be modified is the reporting structure, making the State Police Commissioners to report to the State Governors and the DPO's to report to the LGA Chairmen. All other recommendations remain the same.

REFERENCES

Cochran, John K., Chamlin, Mithcell B., and Seth, Mark (1994).

Deterrence or brutalization? An impact assessment of Oklahoma's return to capital punishment. Criminology 32, 1:107.

George, F. Cole, Christopher E. Smith (2001). The American Criminal Justice System. Wadsworth/Thompson Learning, Belmont, California, USA.

Nigerian Police Force (2004). Library of Congress Country Studies http://1web2.Loc.gob/cgi-bin/query/r?frd/cstdy:@field (DOCIDtng0164)

Kayode, Oluyemi (1976) Public expectations and police role conceptions: Nigeria. The Police Chief, 56-57.

Balogun, Tafa (2004) State Police will destroy national unity — 1G. This Day News, 1-7.

Country Study and County Guide (2002) Nigeria:

Incidence and trends in Crime, 1-4, http://www.lupinfo.com/countryguide-study/nigeria/ nigeria166.html

The Federal Bureau Academy Web (2004). http://www.fbi.gov/hq/td /academy/academy.html

APPENDIX A
NIGERIAN POLICE HEADQUARTERS AND STATE LEVEL RECOMMENDED ORGANIZATIONAL CHART

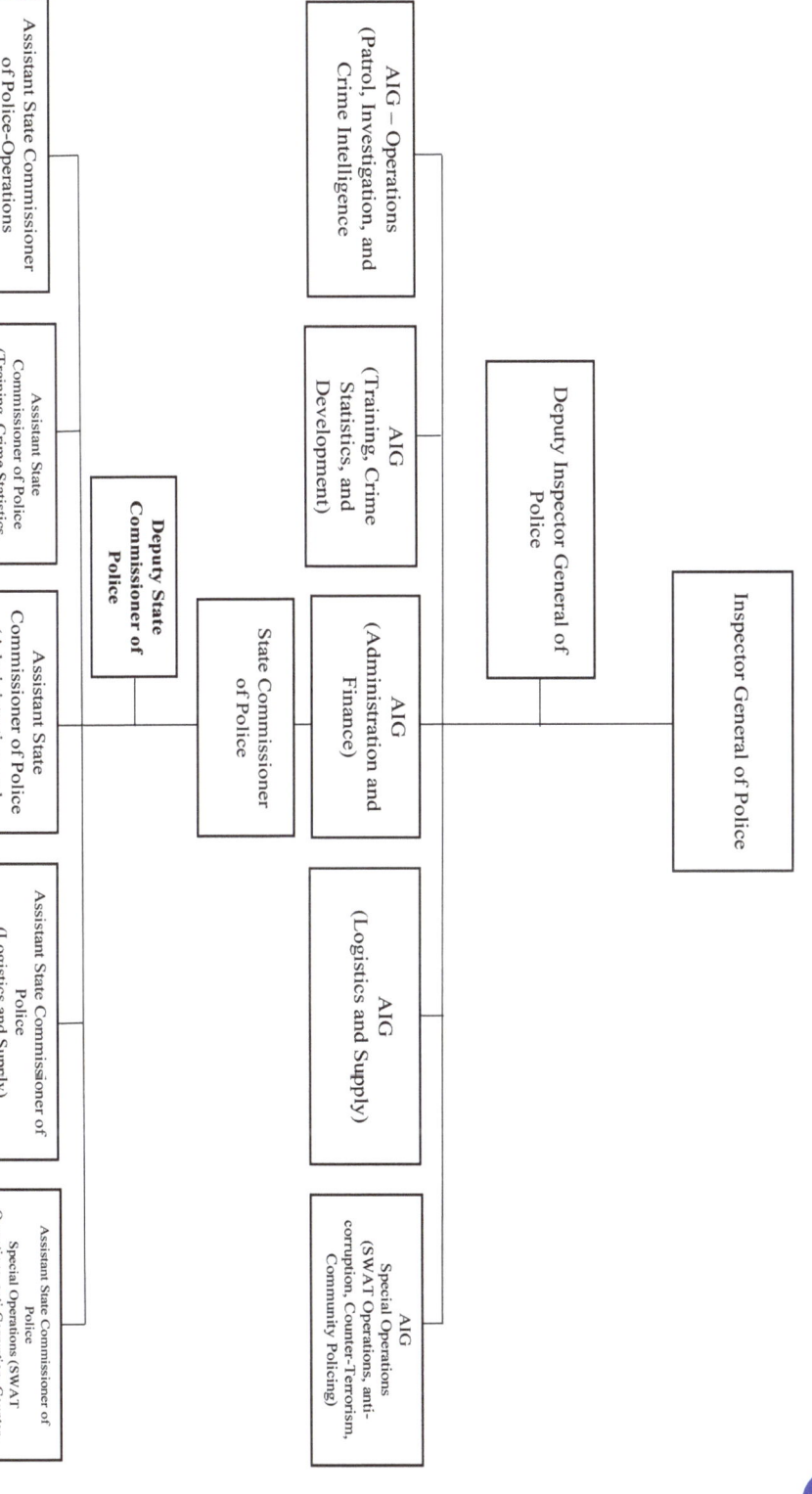

APPENDIX B

NIGERIAN POLICE HEADQUARTERS AND STATE LEVEL RECOMMENDED ORGANIZATIONAL CHART

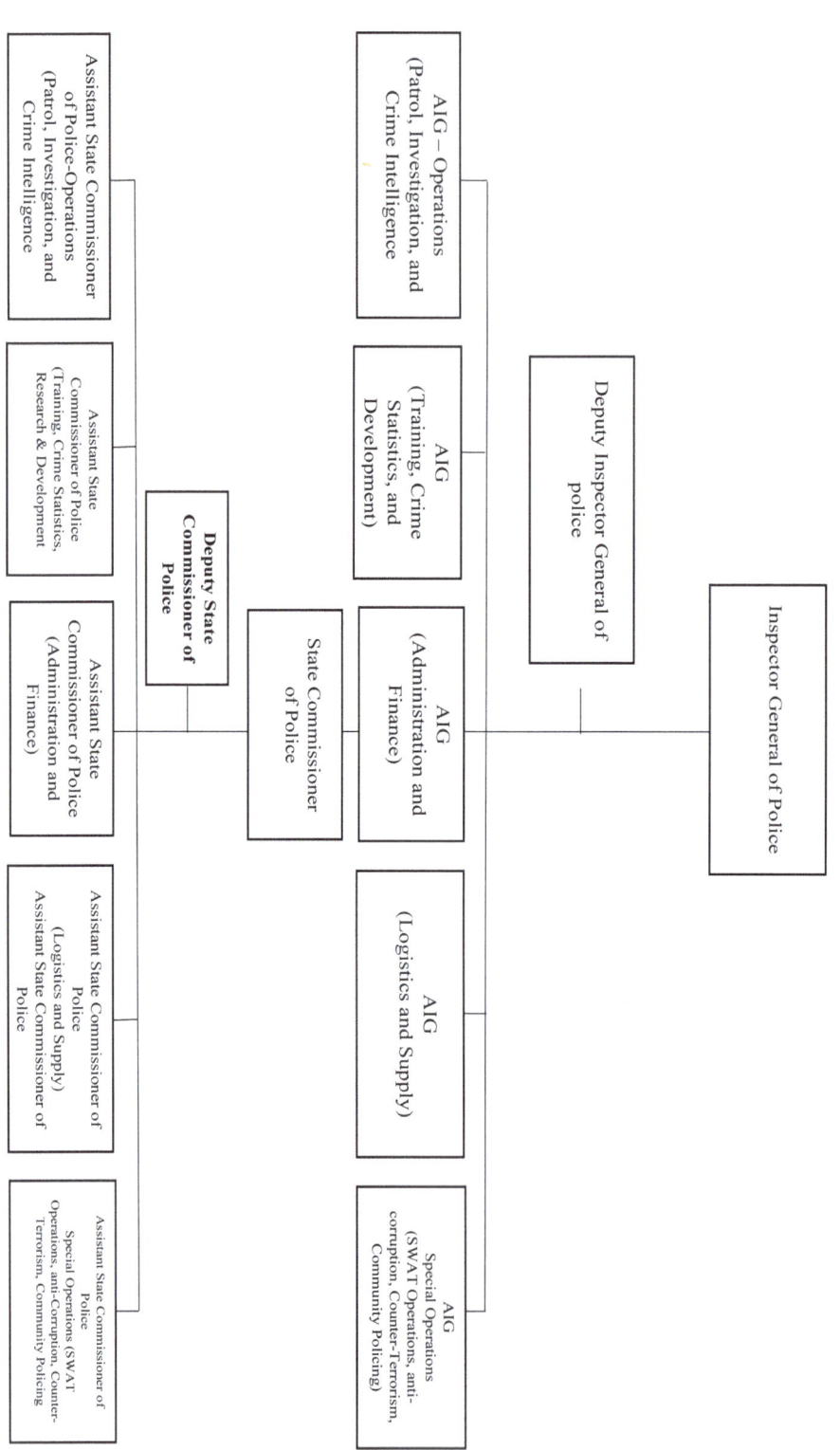

APPENDIX C

VILLAGE LEVEL NIGERIAN POLICE RECOMMENDED ORGANIZATIONAL CHART

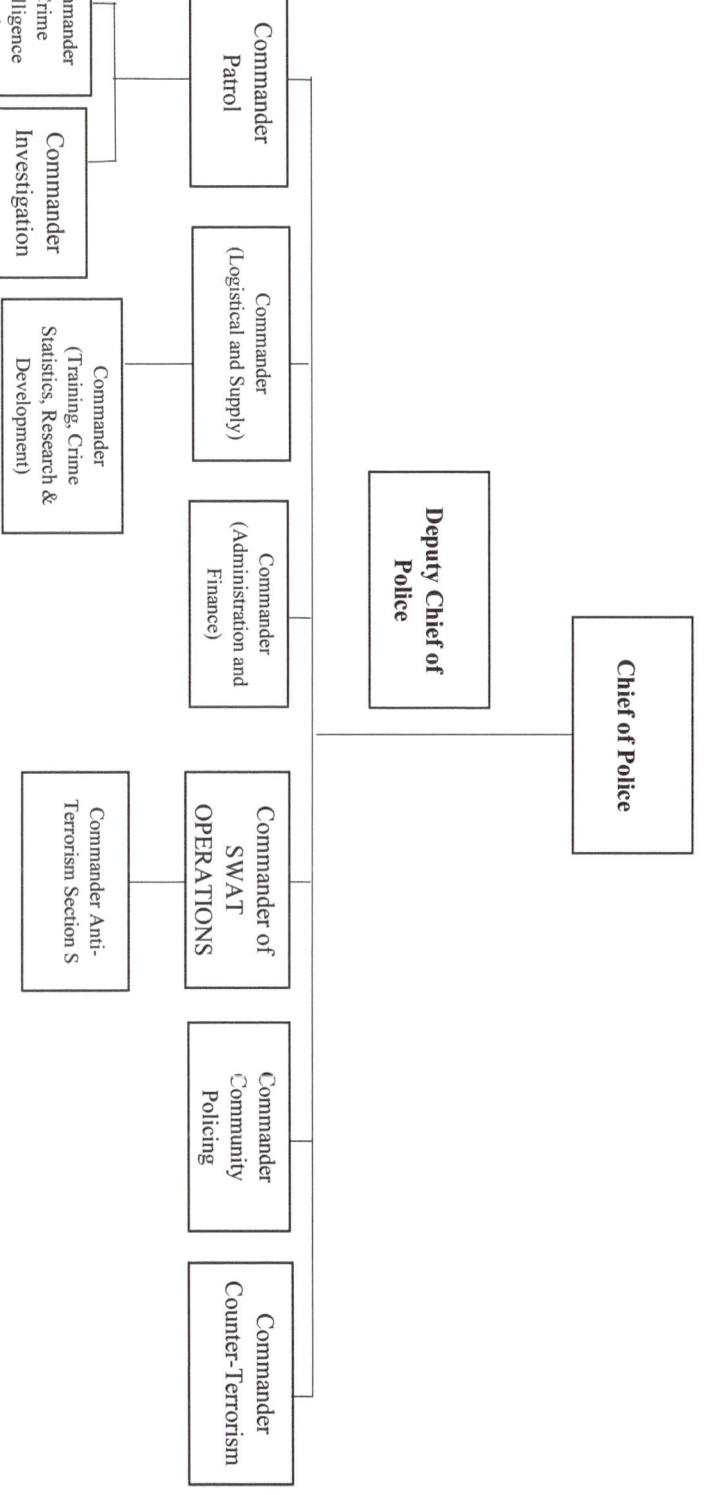

Appendix D City/Town Police Department Personnel

Chief	1 officer
Deputy Chief	1 officer
Assistant Chiefs	5 officers
Patrol	5 officers × 180
Investigation	1 officer × 20
Crime Intelligence	1 officer × 10
Training	1 officer × 5
Research & Development	1 officer × 5
Crime Statistics	1 officer × 5
Administration & Finance	1 officer × 5
Logistics & Supply	1 officer × 5
SWAT	1 officer × 15
Anti Corruption	1 officer × 10
Counter Terrorism	1 officer × 10
Community Policing	1 officer × 10
Clerical Staffs	1 officer × 10
VIP Orderlies	-x 20
Duty Room Dispatch Staff	-x 6
Other	-x 10

TOTAL   24 officers × 326 Rank & File = 350 (Total Strength)

* May be scaled down or up depending on the village size and population.

Appendix "E"

Village Police Department Personnel	
Chief	1 officer
Deputy Chief	1 officer
Patrol	1 officer × 10
Investigation	× 3
Crime Intelligence	1 officer × 5
Training	3
Research & Development	2
Crime Statistics	2
Administration & Finance	1 × 2
Logistics & Supply	× 2
SWAT	1 × 2
Anti Corruption	× 2
Counter Terrorism	× 2
Community Policing	× 2
Clerical Staffs	× 3
VIP Orderlies	× 3
Duty Room Dispatch Staff	× 4

TOTAL 6 officers × 42 = 48 (Total Strength)

* May be scaled down or up depending on the village size and population

Appendix F Police Patrol Car Designated as Per Locality it Serves

Appendix F Police Patrol Car Designated as Per Locality it Serves

Appendix G Police Patrol Car Designated as Per Locality it Serves

ABOUT THE AUTHOR

Professor SALIBA DADDY MUKORO, AN Associate Professor and Head of the Department of Criminal Justice at Mississippi Valley State University, Itta Bena, Mississippi, USA, now the Dean of Graduate School/Professor of Criminal Justice at Jarvis Christian University, has a track record of making near miracles out of reforms. As the Head of the Criminal Justice Department at Mississippi Valley State University, he designed and implemented reforms that moved the department from a fledgling undergraduate program to a strong undergraduate and master's degree programs, with a particularly high enrollment, at the graduate level, second to none in the state of Mississippi, and in some surrounding states. As the staff officer in charge of training at Nigerian Army School of Military Police, he completely reformed the training wing, and designed a reform-oriented Administration and Management course for middle level officers of the Nigeria Police, Nigerian Military Police, Nigerian Air force Police, Nigerian Naval Police, Nigeria Custom Service, and the Nigeria Immigration Service. Some of the course graduates have made it to the top of their services, including the Nigeria Police where some made it to the Assistant Inspector General of Police level, now also to the Inspector General of police position. Professor Saliba Mukoro holds a bachelor's degree in Criminology and Corrections, a master's degree in Criminology and Corrections, and a doctorate degree in Criminal Justice, all from Sam Houston State University, Huntsville, Texas, USA. He is now currently the Dean of Graduate School/Professor of Criminal Justice at Jarvis Christian University, Hawkins Texas.

Printed in the USA
CPSIA information can be obtained
at www.ICGtesting.com
CBHW060005231124
17859CB00013B/91